THE POWER OF A SECOND CHANCE

The Power of a Second Chance

A Love Story

Copyright © 2025 Greg D. Gill & Diana E. Gill

All rights reserved. No part of this publication may be reproduced in a retrieval system, or transmitted in any form or by any means—electronic, mechanical, photocopying, recording, or otherwise—without the prior written permission of the publisher.

Scriptures taken from the Holy Bible, New International Version®, NIV®. Copyright © 1973, 1978, 1984, 2011 by Biblica, Inc.™ Used by permission of Zondervan. All rights reserved worldwide. www.zondervan.com The "NIV" and "New International Version" are trademarks registered in the United States Patent and Trademark Office by Biblica, Inc.™ |

Scripture quotations taken from the (NASB®) New American Standard Bible®, Copyright © 1960, 1971, 1977, 1995, 2020 by The Lockman Foundation. Used by permission. All rights reserved. www.lockman.org. | Scripture quotations taken from the Amplified® Bible (AMP), Copyright © 2015 by The Lockman Foundation. Used by permission. www.lockman.org.

This book is set in the typeface *Athelas* designed by Veronika Burian and Jose Scaglione.

Paperback ISBN: 978-1-967262-37-3

A Publication of *Tall Pine Books*
PO Box 42 Warsaw | Indiana 46581
www.tallpinebooks.com

| 1 25 25 20 16 02 |

Published in the United States of America

THE POWER OF A SECOND CHANCE
A LOVE STORY

BISHOP GREG D. GILL

DIANA E. GILL

Dedicated to our dear friend the Late Pastor Warren Beemer who left us way too soon. He believed in us as a couple and always honoured us with his words, loved us and gave us a kiss on the head.

We miss you.

As a professional Pastoral Counsellor serving lives and especially marriages in crises, it was my honour to walk with Bishop Greg as a friend, colleague, and counsellor during a very difficult and dark time in his life. One of our processes used was *Transformational Principles*, embracing this truth: *"learn to celebrate what you have LEFT, and mourn what you have LOST."* In that way you open the pathway to a future where God can break through and give you a second chance.

This book is all about telling the story of the journey in the Word of God becoming a healing balm and massaging those truths into one's spiritual and emotional being, giving hope and restoration that prepared Diana to meet a man who God had begun a good work in and is faithfully completing still through the process of finding each other after the loss of a spouse. The rest is history... their story will inspire you. You will be blessed by reading this book.

Rev. Simon S. Clarence
Clarence Counselling Centre
Sylvan Lake, Alberta

My wholehearted and long endorsement of the newly released *The Power of a Second Chance: A Love Story*.

I'm a sucker for a good rom-com movie, or a romantic novel of enduring virtue and honour. On any given free evening, there's nothing quite like curling up on a comfy couch with freshly popped popcorn and a hot cup of cocoa to take in a show that stirs and warms the heart!

Personally, I've had the privilege of sitting in a front row seat to watch the incredible love story of Bishop Greg and Diana Gill unfold. I've been held in suspense, in awe, and in delight to see their saga as it moved from loss and loneliness, to answered prayers and a commitment of companionship for a lifetime.

It all started with a pruning. A preparing of hearts.

Everything from their past had been stripped away, due to different circumstances, but the longing was the same for both of them. The deep loneliness had created an empty void, needing to be filled with communion and companionship.

Since creation, God has placed in each of us the need for love and togetherness.

A man is not meant to be alone.

A woman is not meant to be alone.

At Bishop Greg and Diana's unforgettable, exciting wedding, I watched them walk out to the most well-chosen, most fitting wedding song, *"Happy" by Pharrell Williams,* and into their second chance!

The Power of a Second Chance is the powerful display of how God reaches into our broken stories and rewrites the ending with His restorative and redemptive authorship, when we allow Him to.

JENNIFER OSMOND
Author, *Written From My Heart*
Calgary, Alberta

I have had the joy of knowing Bishop Greg and Diana for several years, and in that time I have witnessed the depth of their love, faith, and devotion—not only to each other, but to God and His people. They are a beautiful example of what it means to honour, nurture, and champion one another's gifts.

Their story is one of faith, perseverance, and redemption, and they live it with authenticity and generosity. As a blended family, they have embraced their daughters with remarkable love and unity, and their marriage reflects the grace of a true second chance.

This book will inspire readers to believe again in God's promises, to move forward in faith, and to embrace the power of a second chance with renewed hope.

ROSANGELA ATTE
Certified Christian Life & Brain Coach
Founder & CEO of *The Shift Her Coaching*

I have known Bishop Greg and Lady Di for decades, knowing both of them in their first marriages; watching and hearing firsthand the pain of sickness, death, frustration, grief, and loss. Thank God for new beginnings and second chances.

Because God is gracious and forgiving, we have all experienced the divine redemptive grace—second, third... even hundredth chances. From my vantage point, walking closely with Bishop Greg and Diana in this second chance, a glorious new season, I have witnessed them functioning victoriously in His grace, primarily because of one outstanding character trait.

I have seen a marked propensity toward *teachability*. By that, I don't just mean they know how to take notes and listen well. They have learned how to flex, how to change, how to grow—radically committed to each other, and willing to become more like Jesus as they contend for their marriage and for each other. Obviously, no marriage is perfect! But where there is good communication, tender hearts, and—very crucially—a teachable spirit, anything can happen. I pray that you will be encouraged by their divinely inspired lessons, but please know: if you remain flexible and teachable, with a tender heart, God can do precisely what He desires to do in your heart and life!

Rev. D. Mark Griffin
Friend and Brother of the Gills

I've had the privilege of knowing Bishop Greg and Diana for over 30 years, first as two unique and incredible individuals, and then as an even more remarkable couple. I witnessed Bishop Greg's unwavering loyalty to his faith and dedication to ministry long before Diana entered the picture, and I also saw Diana's tireless commitment and infectious optimism before God brought her a new partner to share it with. To watch those two forces come together—to see how their strengths have magnified one another over the decades—has been an absolute joy.

This book offers a glimpse into the kind of enduring partnership that can only be built on a foundation of deep individual character, and I cannot think of a better couple to illustrate that truth.

LISA (LISE) LANSUE
Friend of Bishop and Lady Di

I am honoured to endorse Bishop Greg and Diana Gill's book, a powerful testament to their transformative journey from brokenness to restoration. As a couple who has been married since 2014, they are living proof of the profound impact that occurs when God's love and grace are at the forefront of a relationship.

Both Bishop Greg and Diana have overcome past relationships marked by hurt and pain, and their story is a hopeful example of redemption. Through their faith in

God, they have not only healed individually but have also discovered a deeper, more meaningful connection with each other. Their marriage expresses hope to others, demonstrating the transformative power of trusting in God to restore and renew not only individual hearts but also love and commitment.

Bishop Greg and Diana offer readers more than just a personal narrative; they provide a powerful testament to the human capacity for healing and restoration. Their story encourages others to trust in God's transformative power, inspiring them to build stronger, more loving relationships.

This book will inspire, equip, and empower those who have faced adversity in their relationships, offering practical wisdom and encouragement. I wholeheartedly endorse it for anyone seeking hope, healing, and guidance in their own relationship journey.

CARLOS SARMIENTO
Orlando House of Prayer

I have had the privilege of witnessing Bishop Greg and Lady Di live out the very message they are sharing in this book. Their journey is not just words on a page—it is a testimony of grace, resilience, and the redeeming power of God's love.

What has always stood out to me is not just their love for each other, but their unwavering hope in God. I have seen them face real-life challenges with honesty and faith, and I have also seen them rise with strength, humility, and joy. Their story is proof that second chances are not only possible, but they can be more beautiful than the first dream.

This book is not only their love story—it is an invitation for all of us to believe again in God's faithfulness, in healing, and in the promise of a future filled with hope.

CHRISTINE MARTIN
Friend of Bishop and Lady Di

In this deeply moving memoir, Bishop Greg Gill and Diana Gill share their journey through heartbreak and healing—one through the loss of a beloved husband to cancer, the other through the pain of divorce. Together, they discover the quiet power of second chances and the unexpected beauty of new beginnings. Honest, tender, and full of hope, this book is a reminder that even after life breaks us, love can rebuild us. *"I would have despaired unless I had believed that I would see the goodness of the Lord in the land of the living."* — *Psalm 27:13 (NASB)*

Rev. Ben Adekugbe
President, *Barnabas Agenda*

I like to selfishly believe that Bishop Greg's and Lady Diana's relationship would never have come about if it wasn't for me. After all, if I had not invited the Bishop to come to Edmonton and join me in attending the *Breakforth* conference in January of 2013, the chance meeting of these two beautiful souls may never have happened. However, I know that this couple was ordained by God Himself to be together, and His will would have come forth with or without my intervention.

I will always remember how broken and discouraged my good friend was when his first marriage dissolved. I walked through many dark days with him when he felt like he could not continue and that his future was uncertain. Although I did not know Lady Diana and her story during these times, I came to realize how her life was also in such disarray after the death of her first husband. God sure knew what He was doing when He brought these two broken people together.

Over the years I have watched Bishop Greg and Lady Diana's relationship grow and strengthen on a daily basis. The relationship has not been without its trials and tribulations along the way, but with the power of the Holy Spirit working in and through them both, they have walked through and overcome everything that the enemy has tried to throw at them to cause discord and divide.

This book will encourage you to seek the power of the Holy Spirit in your life and relationships. And remember that God is not finished with you yet. He is and always will be the God of Second Chances—and much more!

Kevin Kirby
Friend of Bishop Greg and Lady Di

CONTENTS

Foreword	xix
Introduction	xxiii

PART ONE
BREAKING & WILDERNESS

1. Death and Divorce	3
2. Loneliness, Tears, and the Unknown	11

PART TWO
SPARKS & PREPARATION

3. Courage to Start Over	21
4. Preparation for the New	27

PART THREE
COVENANT & BLENDING

5. It Is Well — The Wedding	35
6. Blended = Counselling	41

PART FOUR
ON MISSION & UPHEAVAL

7. A Whole New World	49
8. Covid and Minimalism	55

PART FIVE
GRIEF AGAIN & RESILIENCE

9. Loved Ones Lost	63
10. Renewing of Vows and Rebuilding	69

PART SIX
YOUR SECOND CHANCE

11. What Does Your Second Chance Look Like?	77
Conclusion and Summary	81
Also by Bishop Greg D. Gill and Diana E. Gill	87

FOREWORD

I am honoured to write this foreword for the book "The Power of a Second Chance: A Love Story", which chronicles the journey of two remarkable individuals, Bishop Greg and Diana Gill.

Bishop Greg and I first met over thirty-five years ago during our Bible College days. It would be some time later before I had the privilege of meeting Diana.

We all begin life with dreams, hopes, and plans for a future filled with love, laughter, and purpose—a life full of victories and vicarious experiences. Rarely do we consider the possibility of heartbreak, loss, or unforeseen sorrow. For many years, Bishop Greg and Diana lived that dream. They were content, joyful, and living lives filled with promise.

But then came the unexpected.

Diana's life was forever altered when her husband succumbed to illness, leaving her a young widow. Suddenly, her world was turned upside down. Grief, uncertainty, and loneliness became constant companions as she found herself navigating the uncharted path of single parenthood. The joy she once knew was replaced with pain, and anger began to knock at her heart daily. She wrestled with questions that had no easy answers.

Bishop Greg, meanwhile, was pastoring a vibrant, growing congregation. On the surface, life appeared to be thriving. But behind closed doors, his world was quietly unraveling. He endured the pain of a broken marriage, the shame of separation, and ultimately, the heartbreak of divorce. The future he had envisioned seemed to collapse around him. He felt disqualified, convinced that his ministry—and perhaps even his purpose—was over. Who would want to hear from a pastor whose own life had fallen apart?

Neither Bishop Greg nor Diana planned for these detours. Their life compasses seemed broken, offering no clear direction. Yet, even in their pain and uncertainty, God was still at work. Quietly, faithfully, He was orchestrating a story of redemption. Their individual journeys, marked by brokenness and loss, began to converge. Where despair once lived, hope began to rise. Where there was sorrow, joy began to return.

In "The Power of a Second Chance: A Love Story," you

will read about this beautiful journey of healing and restoration. You'll witness how God took the shattered pieces of two lives and gently began to rebuild them—not only individually, but together. This book is more than a love story between two people. It is a testimony of God's grace, His faithfulness, and His power to redeem even our most painful chapters.

As you turn the pages, you'll experience their past, be inspired by their present, and look with hope toward their future. This is a story of healing. A story of redemption. A story of moving forward.

Most of all, it is a story of a second chance.

Rev. Deano R. Young
Dip. Th, B.Th, MBC, DPC (Hon)
CPMHC-GP

INTRODUCTION

Life goes by so quickly. We all make plans and dream dreams, but sometimes life does not go as we hoped. At twenty years old, we feel like we can conquer the world—but what if things don't go our way? What if circumstances unravel, leaving us with hurt, pain, and disillusionment? How do we keep moving forward? How do we believe in hope? How do we learn to trust again?

Greg and I met during a time when life was full and exciting. We believed the best for each other and had hope for the future. But then everything crumbled. Our paths separated, and each of us was left to wander and wonder: *What's next? Would we dare dream again? Could we believe that there could be more?*

God was, and still is, at the center of it all. He knows the beginning from the end and every step in between.

When we are born, we are new and unscathed. Our parents pour into us, teaching us what they have learned. They guide us into adulthood, often through their own stories of pain, sorrow, and perseverance. Through it all, they encourage us to serve God and trust Him.

When we put our hope in God and allow Him to walk with us daily—teaching us one step at a time—He will lead us. He will bring us to where He wants us to be and to the people He wants in our lives. He is faithful, and His desire is to bless us.

> *"May God himself, the God of peace, sanctify you through and through. May your whole spirit, soul, and body be kept blameless at the coming of our Lord Jesus Christ. The one who calls you is faithful, and He will do it."*
> — **1 Thessalonians 5:23–24**

> *"For I know the plans I have for you," declares the Lord, "plans to prosper you and not to harm you, plans to give you hope and a future."* — **Jeremiah 29:11**

If we truly believe this, then we must also believe we have both hope and a future.

The next verse reminds us:

> *"Then you will call on me and come and pray to me, and I will listen to you."* — **Jeremiah 29:12**

When life falls apart and we don't know what to do, God invites us to call on Him. And when we do, He promises to be with us.

Greg and I were married on August 15, 2014. Our story is a testimony of God's grace—a second chance. We had faith that He was with us, and He continues to walk with us still.

We want this book to give hope to you, wherever you are on your journey. Each of us faces pain, regret, sorrow, and broken dreams at some point in life. But listen to the words of Jesus:

> "I have told you these things, so that in me you may have peace. In this world you will have trouble. But take heart! I have overcome the world." — **John 16:33**

Be encouraged, even when the pain feels too deep, God is at work behind the scenes. Many of the trials we face are preparing us for a new chapter we never imagined possible.

Throughout this book, you'll hear from both Greg's perspective and Diana's. We want you to see where we were each coming from, what we were thinking, and how God's hand was guiding us. He brought things together beyond our imagination.

"Now to him who is able to do immeasurably more than all we ask or imagine, according to his power that is at work within us." — **Ephesians 3:20**

This is our story, but it's also an invitation for you to believe that God can do the same in your life. We want to share it with you for wherever you are in your life. Thank you for allowing us to share and we hope that you will be encouraged. Take time to reflect at the end of each chapter with some of your own notes and a guided prayer. Whether you are reading this as our friends, our family or getting to know us for the first time or perhaps you are looking for your second chance.

REFLECTION

- Where in your story have you faced broken dreams or unexpected detours?
- Can you identify a moment when God was quietly working behind the scenes?
- What part of your journey do you need to trust Him with today?

PRAYER

Father, thank You for being faithful even when my life feels uncertain.

Help me to see that my story isn't over—that You are still writing new chapters.

Teach me to trust You with my broken places and to believe in the hope and future You have promised.

I choose to surrender my heart to You and believe that You can bring beauty from ashes.

Amen.

PART ONE
BREAKING & WILDERNESS

CHAPTER 1
DEATH AND DIVORCE

DIANA

Two words that do not bring hope, but only sadness: death and divorce. Both marked the end of our first marriages. Not by our choice, not by our desire. We had each planned to be married to the same person for many, many years. But here we were, our lives turned upside down.

Greg was separated and then divorced after fourteen years of marriage. I (Diana) lost my husband, Dave, to cancer after twenty-one years together.

In many ways, our lives were similar. We both grew up in the same denomination—attending Sunday school, Sunday night services, Bible camp, Crusaders, youth group, and even serving in youth ministry.

That's actually how we first met. We were both married, both serving God, both wanting the best for our families and ministries. Greg was the youth camp speaker, and Dave and I attended as a couple. Later, Greg invited us to a young adult conference where we were poured into and encouraged. Over the years we kept in touch occasionally, though eventually life carried us to different places.

Dave and I faced years of illness as he battled cancer. In his final days, a friend reached out to Greg to let him know what was happening. Greg prayed for Dave's healing while also sending me encouragement. When Dave finally breathed his last, I walked out of the hospital a forty-one-year-old widow. My life as I knew it had ended in a moment.

Greg reached out with this message:

"Di, just got your post. My deepest sympathies to you and the family. I do not understand these things. Props to you for the fight and bold stand you took for healing right to the end. I am so proud of y'all. May Holy Spirit come and comfort you and guide you into His peace and love at this your time of need. Love you much! Bless you, Giller."

The days that followed were a blur. We planned a funeral within five days. It was November, and Christmas was approaching. Each "first" was painful—

the first birthday, first Christmas, first New Year's without Dave.

During that time, Greg would check in and encourage me through Facebook Messenger. He carried a burden for me. I once commented on a picture of his beautiful family, only to learn he had been separated for three and a half years. My heart broke for him.

Two months after Dave's death, my father passed away. Greg sent condolences again, hardly able to believe what I was walking through. Grief was overwhelming, but by the four-month mark I began to believe there might be more ahead. In faith, I wrote out a list of what I hoped for in a future husband. I was still grieving, but I also felt a spark of new hope—a dream for something beyond the pain.

GREG

I found myself alone, still wanting to minister, but feeling unworthy. *How can I preach when I'm going through a marriage breakup? Who would want to listen to me?*

In my book *I Will Not: Pursuing the Path to Perseverance*, I share more about this season. God opened doors and placed people in my life who believed in me and helped me believe in myself. My dream had been to plant a church—and I did—but that's when separation came.

I remember God whispering to my heart: *"Your dream*

was to pastor one hundred and fifty people, but I want you to pastor the world."

It was not what I expected, but God was calling me to the nations. Even in my despair, He still had a plan.

Meanwhile, I prayed for my marriage to be restored, though the divorce moved steadily forward. I was heartbroken. Still, God reminded me that my story was not over. He even sent a young man into my life who was walking through his own divorce, and I was able to encourage him while I was hurting myself.

When I heard that Dave was dying, I felt a strong burden for Diana. I prayed for her and checked in from time to time. A year after Dave's death, I reached out again, knowing the anniversary would be especially difficult.

That's when I learned she would be at a conference. At first, I didn't plan to attend. But then a friend unexpectedly offered me a ticket. It was three hours away, but I felt God nudging me to go.

I messaged Diana to confirm she would be there, still with no romantic inclination. I was too broken to think that way.

At the conference, we saw each other for the first time in about eight years. We hugged as friends and sat together during a session. Later, we ended up at the same restaurant, talking with friends. I had no idea what God was doing. A second chance wasn't even on my mind.

DIANA

When Greg told me he'd be at the conference, I was excited. It had been years. I went back to my hotel, fixed my hair, and changed my outfit—I wanted to look my best. When I hugged him, I held on a little longer than usual.

We introduced each other to our friends. But despite his pain, Greg still prayed for people, prophesied, and carried the anointing of God.

At the restaurant, though, I was a little disappointed—he mostly ate spaghetti, chatted with his friend, and watched the hockey game. I wanted to connect, to know where he really was in life. Still, something stirred in my heart.

The next day we were texting back and forth throughout the day. I enjoyed the friendship and the conversation. Later that night, we drove together and finally had space to talk deeply. He shared his heartbreak, his dreams, and his hopes for the future. Quietly, I thought: *I could be that person for him.*

That night, as he spoke, I felt the presence of the Holy Spirit like a swirl across the table. Something was shifting.

That week, we began talking on the phone every night. It felt like having company again. Friendship was slowly becoming something more.

GREG

During this time, a friend asked me, *"What would make you happy?"*

I answered honestly: "Getting my marriage back."

But then he asked me a question that stayed with me: *"What if God has a different plan?"*

That question was a turning point. God was gently showing me that He was leading me into something I never expected. Diana and I were both broken, both grieving different kinds of losses—but slowly, I began to see God might be writing a new chapter.

DIANA

When I traveled to Arizona, Greg and I continued to talk —sometimes into the early hours of the morning on video calls. My heart was turning. Was it okay to love again? Could I move forward?

God's plan was unfolding. Step by step, He was showing me that it was safe to trust Him with a new beginning.

One night I blurted out the words, "I love you!" Greg wasn't ready to say it back, but I had to speak it. It was where my heart was.

Soon after, I listened to one of Dave's old sermons. In it, he spoke of Job:

"Job's life was more blessed the second time around."

As I heard those words, I wept. It felt like God—and even Dave—were giving me permission to embrace this second chance.

REFLECTION

- Where in your life have you experienced loss or brokenness that seemed final?
- Do you believe God could write a "second chance" story for you too?
- What fears or hesitations might be holding you back from new hope?

PRAYER

Dear Lord,

Thank You for my life and for the gift of new beginnings. You see my heart and all of its longings. I choose to trust You with my future, believing that You have hope and restoration ahead for me.

Give me courage to step into Your plan with faith.

In Jesus' name, Amen.

CHAPTER 2
LONELINESS, TEARS, AND THE UNKNOWN

DIANA

The bus ride home gave me too much time to think. My heart felt like it was on the outside of my chest, torn between grief and a fragile new hope. One moment I laughed, the next I cried. Grief was still so vivid.

My daughters were grieving too, missing their dad. And I was missing my partner in life. By then, all three of my girls had moved out, leaving me alone in a five-bedroom house with three dogs and four cats. I tried to fill the emptiness by renovating—painting, replacing carpet, even updating the bathroom. Anything to get the house ready to sell. I couldn't face another lonely winter there.

In the midst of this, Greg and I continued talking—video chats, emails, texts, and Facebook messages. He constantly encouraged me, prayed for me, and spoke life into me. Before long, I even began helping him with administrative tasks, something I loved. One of those was his visa application for a mission trip to Pakistan.

That's when a detail stopped me in my tracks. The application asked for his parents' full names. Greg gave me his father's: *David Charles*. My late husband's name was also *David Charles*. And Greg's middle name? David.

I couldn't believe it. These were little "kisses from God" that reminded me He was weaving something bigger than I could see.

GREG

Valentine's Day was approaching, and I felt torn. I wasn't officially in a relationship, and yet, was I? My heart was being stirred in new ways.

A trusted friend advised me to acknowledge the day—not with full romance, but as a gesture of friendship. I called a flower shop in Diana's town and ordered a dozen long-stemmed red roses. On the card, I signed: *"Your friend, Greg."*

It felt like a small step of faith.

DIANA

When the roses arrived, I was undone. Tears streamed as I realized how much it meant. For years, flowers had come from one man, and now—suddenly—from another. The bouquet became a symbol of release and of possibility.

That evening my daughter Alicia and her husband stopped by. They saw the roses and the look on my face, and Alicia laughed: *"She's twitter-pated!"* (a word from Disney's *Bambi*). She wasn't wrong.

That night, I gave Alicia two of Dave's rings—his wedding ring and our fifteenth anniversary ring. Handing them to her felt like another step of letting go.

I soon left to visit my mom in Manitoba, meeting my brother Laurence in Winnipeg to travel together. Family time was healing. At the hotel, I worked on editing Dave's unfinished book, *Getting Well at Being Sick*. He had written eleven chapters before he died, and I was determined to finish it.

As we talked, my family gently wondered aloud what it might look like if I ever met someone new. Laurence and I caught each other's eyes—we both knew I already had. Explaining it was hard. Explaining it to myself was harder.

This is where fear creeps in. Not everyone understands second chances. Especially after death or divorce, people often think they know better. But at the end of the day, it was between me and God. His Word in Jeremiah 29:11 reminded me that His plans were to prosper me, not to harm me.

Still, friends and family were cautious. They didn't want me hurt again. And Greg was facing the same thing—his friends wanted to check me out, just as mine wanted to check him out.

GREG

I only shared about Diana with people I deeply trusted. Honestly, I was scared—still trying to believe this was real. Often, when I introduced her, it was over the phone so friends could hear her voice and heart.

One friend had known Diana and Dave years earlier. When he learned about us, he was thrilled. He told me he felt the Holy Spirit on it and gave us his full blessing. That meant a lot.

In March, I invited Diana to Ontario with me to visit friends and family. She stayed with a high school friend while I visited my parents and extended family. We had countless coffee dates, dinners, and meetings. We were cautious, not knowing how people would react.

To my relief, most were excited. My aunt, who had just lost her husband, welcomed Diana warmly. She didn't want to see me hurt again but could clearly see God's hand in this new relationship. My cousins were curious too. They had seen how low I had been and were grateful to see hope returning.

In April, I had the opportunity to preach in Saskatchewan—close to where Diana and her daughters lived. It gave me a chance to meet her girls. That was stretching for them, as it should be. I didn't want to replace their dad, but I wanted them to know I cared.

Some of Diana's friends attended the meetings too. While many were encouraged, others weren't so sure. That's part of walking out a second chance—it can be misunderstood. All we could do was pray, trust God, and keep moving forward.

That month was also Diana's birthday. I surprised her with a weekend trip to Edmonton. We shared dinners with friends, attended a house church, and even went shopping. I gave her seven birthday cards to open at different times over the weekend—a tradition I still love.

DIANA

At my home church, the pastors had resigned, and the board was interviewing candidates. I told them I was planning to move to Alberta and offered to let the new pastors privately view my house before it went on the market.

While I attended Alicia's baby shower in Calgary that

May, the new pastors decided to buy my house directly. No listings, no open houses, no strangers wandering through my space. For a widow, that kind of protection mattered. God was taking care of details I couldn't.

The next step was finding a new house in Calgary. Since I couldn't leave while waiting for my grandson's birth, I sent Greg my wish list and asked him to help. He went with a realtor—whose last name, fittingly, was *Hope*.

GREG

We looked at several homes, but the first one stood out. When we returned for a second look, something clicked. Everywhere we turned, we saw purple—her favorite color. A purple toaster, purple chairs, purple KitchenAid mixer, purple pillows, even purple flowers on the porch. I emailed her a picture of that toaster with one word: *SOLD*.

I knew this was her house. And she trusted me enough to believe it too.

By July, Diana's move to Calgary was set. I was thrilled, though still nervous, not knowing what lay ahead.

DIANA

On July 3rd, my first grandson was born. Holding him in my arms was pure joy. A few days later, we traveled so my mom and Dave's mom could meet him. We captured four generations in photos—a precious moment that would never come again.

Soon after, Greg and I went to Ontario so I could meet his parents. Greg's dad was a die-hard Montreal Canadiens fan—the Habs. I wanted to make a memorable first impression, so I bought a Habs jersey in Toronto and wore it to our dinner at Red Lobster.

When Greg's dad walked in and saw me in that jersey, he grinned from ear to ear. I handed him a Habs hat as a gift, while I gave Greg's mom a bracelet and scarf. We all laughed, shared a meal, and these beautiful people got to know me. Our second chance was unfolding and becoming very real.

REFLECTION

"The fig tree forms its early fruit; the blossoming vines spread their fragrance. Arise, come, my darling; my beautiful one, come with me." — **Song of Songs 2:13 (NIV)**

1. What does your fear look like right now?
2. How might your family respond to a new chapter in your life?
3. Will you trust God with the details?

PRAYER

Dear Lord,
    There are so many moving parts to moving on. Please be with every detail and give me the courage to believe You hold my life in Your hands.
    In Jesus' name, Amen.

PART TWO
SPARKS & PREPARATION

CHAPTER 3
COURAGE TO START OVER

DIANA

When I announced to my church that I was moving to Calgary, it felt like stepping into the unknown. God's timing was clear: after a year without a pastor, the new pastoral couple arrived—and they even bought my house. I knew the Lord was guiding the transition.

My daughter Alicia and her husband had already secured a job in Calgary, and with my newborn grandson, they would be moving with me—living in the basement until they found their own place. My other two daughters, however, would be staying behind. That goodbye was heartbreaking. When I hugged my youngest, just seventeen, I cried. Starting over always involves sacrifice.

With my nephew Nicholas driving the moving truck, we hauled all our belongings ten hours west. I had never even seen the house in person. It was an act of trust. The night before possession, we stayed in a hotel, and I tried to keep my nerves steady.

Then came a wave of stress over the closing costs. Panic rose up. Greg was in Ontario with his daughters, and I called him in tears. We prayed together over the phone, refusing to let fear win. By the next day, everything was finalized. At noon, I held the keys to my new home. My realtor and broker even took me to lunch to celebrate. When I walked through that front door, I knew: my Calgary adventure had begun.

GREG

I was nervous. Diana had just moved to my city, trusting God with countless details that still weren't fully worked out. I wasn't sure how long it would take for everything to settle, but I admired her courage.

At the time, I was meeting weekly with a small group in a business center, planting the seeds of a new church. Diana offered to open her home for those gatherings. It became a natural way for her to meet the people connected to me—and eventually, for my daughters to get to know her.

To my relief, my girls loved her right away. She won them over with puzzles and chocolates, and before long, they were laughing together. My heart stretched with all the newness.

We launched the church in her living room and gathered every week, learning as we went. One of the highlights was dedicating Diana's grandson, Jude, to the Lord. My daughters came, one of Diana's daughters joined, and for the first time, our families began blending.

Later, I sat down with my older girls to share openly that I had feelings for Diana. They had already figured it out—but hearing their support still meant the world. It was both painful and healing, stretching me in ways I hadn't expected.

DIANA

Once the boxes were unpacked and pictures hung, my new house felt like home. But leaving behind ten years of memories wasn't easy. Even with excitement, change comes with grief. It felt like birthing pains, painful to endure, but leading to something new.

I still owned rental properties in Nipawin, ten hours away, and managing them from a distance was difficult. On top of that, I felt the need to work again. I had been with the bank for years before Dave passed away, so I decided to apply at financial institutions in Calgary.

It was harder than I expected. The memories connected to the bank—Dave's hospital trips, his death—were overwhelming. I cried as I filled out applications. Still, I pressed through. At the interview, the hiring manager showed such kindness, encouraging me to simply visit one branch and see how it felt. That branch was five minutes from my house.

I met with the assistant manager for an hour and a half—and didn't realize it would spark a friendship that still lasts. I got the job. Even the parking lot was angled just like the one in my small town. Little touches of familiarity reminded me: God was taking care of me.

I was also getting to know Greg better, learning his daughters' rhythms, and finding my place in this new city life.

Soon, my middle daughter, Jessica, visited, pregnant with my second grandson. She came for Jude's baby dedication and met Greg's daughters. Later, my youngest, Christa, moved to Calgary with her boyfriend, and suddenly my house was full again—two daughters, their partners, and a grandson all under one roof.

My first Christmas in Calgary was memorable. Greg's mom and nieces visited, and I met more of his extended family. The holidays were bittersweet—joy mixed with memories—but hope was taking root.

Starting over is like two trains that had been derailed, now trying to join tracks and move forward together. It's exciting but also challenging. Still, I trusted that God had every detail in His hands.

REFLECTION

"See, I am doing a new thing! Now it springs up; do you not perceive it? I am making a way in the wilderness and streams in the wasteland." — **Isaiah 43:19**

1. What might your "new" look like?
2. What pulls at your heart the most as you move forward?
3. Which holiday brings the deepest memories for you—and why?

PRAYER

Dear Lord,

You make all things new in Your time.

Please help me with each step of change, and give me peace as I let go of the past.

I trust You with what's ahead.

In Jesus' name, Amen.

CHAPTER 4
PREPARATION FOR THE NEW

DIANA

The new year had arrived, and I knew it was time to prepare for what was next. So many moving parts, so many daughters, and so much change ahead. I shared with my girls that marriage could be in the future, and I also let Dave's mom know. She was excited for me. Having lived her own second chances, she wanted to celebrate mine. Sadly, her health declined, and by March 2014, she passed away. I attended the funeral, honoured to share a few words about how much she had meant to me.

Soon after, I celebrated my 44th birthday. Greg surprised me with 44 roses and dinner with my girls. We were waiting for the right time as a couple, and some days the waiting felt heavy. Fear, doubt, and frustration crept in, but we kept reminding ourselves to focus on God's plan.

We already had a wedding date in mind, but the engagement hadn't yet happened. Greg was away speaking in San Antonio, and while he was gone, I went dress shopping. God left His little "kisses" for me again—reminders that He was in the details. The shop was called *David's Bridal*, the clerk's name was Jessica (two of our daughters share that name), and I found a dress that fit perfectly. It all felt like confirmation that God was leading the way.

GREG

While I was in San Antonio, I was invited to speak at a women's meeting. The Holy Spirit prompted me to share about Diana's journey as a widow and how she had chosen to write down five things she was thankful for each day.

> *"Rejoice always, pray continually, give thanks in all circumstances; for this is God's will for you in Christ Jesus."*
> — **1 Thessalonians 5:16–18**

The women were deeply moved, and at the end of my message, I told them that when I returned home, I planned to ask this widow to marry me. The place erupted in cheers! It was bold to share something so personal, but I felt God's courage rising in me.

The only problem was money—I wanted to take Diana to a nice dinner, but I didn't have the funds. Then I remembered my washer and dryer, which I could sell. Diana listed them online, and they sold almost immediately. God had provided exactly what was needed for our special night.

I decided Mother's Day would be the right day to propose.

DIANA

When the washer and dryer sold so quickly, I laughed—it was just in time. On Mother's Day, after working, I bought myself a new dress "just in case." Greg looked so handsome in his jacket and button-up shirt.

We had a lovely steak dinner and I thought nothing more would happen that night. Greg said he didn't have the ring with him, and I let myself believe it. Then dessert was ordered—a slice of cheesecake—and before it came, Greg began reading a poem.

The poem told our story—our pasts, our heartbreaks, and the way God had brought us together. And then came the words:

"I need you to know my love for you is real...

My question to you is, 'Will you marry me?'"

I said yes. At that moment, the waitress brought the cheesecake—with the ring sitting on top, gleaming in the light.

We took photos, shared the news with our daughters, and posted it to social media. It shocked everyone—but filled our hearts with joy. The waiting was over. Now it was time to plan a wedding.

Just days later, my second grandson was born. I traveled to Saskatchewan to hold tiny Scotty in my arms and celebrate with my daughter. Life was moving quickly—new life, new love, new beginnings. Through it all, God was faithful.

Where are you right now? Maybe your life feels upside down. Maybe the future hasn't gone as planned. You can stay stuck in regret, or you can rise up and walk into the new that God has for you.

REFLECTION AND PRAYER

> *"Not that I have already obtained all this, or have already arrived at my goal, but I press on to take hold of that for which Christ Jesus took hold of me. Brothers and sisters, I do not consider myself yet to have taken hold of it.*
>
> *But one thing I do: Forgetting what is behind and straining toward what is ahead, I press on toward the goal to*

win the prize for which God has called me heavenward in Christ Jesus." — **Philippians 3:12–14 NIV**

1. What are some things you need to say goodbye to?
2. Can you be fully present in this season, and what do you appreciate most right now?
3. What five things are you thankful for today?

PRAYER

Dear Lord,

Sometimes it's hard to let go of the past, and sometimes it's a fight to keep pressing on.

Thank You for the promise of new beginnings.

Help me to believe that You have good things ahead for me.

In Jesus' name, Amen.

PART THREE
COVENANT & BLENDING

CHAPTER 5
IT IS WELL — THE WEDDING

DIANA

I had to decide who would walk me down the aisle. My dad had passed away only two months after Dave. We chose August 15th for the wedding day—it would have been my dad's birthday.

At first, I thought of asking one of my brothers, or even a close friend, but in the end I felt to walk down on my own. My four bridesmaids told the story of my life: one childhood friend, one from Saskatoon, one from Nipawin, and one I had met in Calgary. Each represented a chapter of my journey, and together they celebrated what God was doing.

Moving forward means making choices that not everyone will agree with. Opinions abound. It takes courage, strength, and the wisdom to surround yourself with people who love and support you. Some will not come along for the ride, but you still have to keep moving forward. God's plan for your life may not look like what you imagined, but His purposes are still unfolding.

As the bridesmaids walked down the aisle, followed by our daughters, the song *"It Is Well"* began to play.

Through it all, through it all
My eyes are on You
And it is well with me.

When I reached the end of the aisle, we lifted our hands together in worship. Tears ran down my face. This was only possible because of faith—because we knew God was with us.

GREG

My groomsmen were men who had walked with me through thick and thin. Their friendship had been a lifeline, and it was an honour to have them beside me that day. A dear pastor friend performed the ceremony, while others gathered around us in prayer.

I was both scared and excited. Starting over felt unknown, and fear tried to creep in, but faith pushed us forward. Family and friends surrounded us, cheering us on. My friend Pastor Warren Beemer summed it up beautifully in his speech: *"We prayed for Greg, and Diana is the answer to our prayers."*

Then my daughters spoke. Even my six-year-old shared: *"Diana, since the first day I met you, you changed my life!"* There wasn't a dry eye in the room. Seeing my girls embrace Diana, after all the pain they had endured, brought me great joy and peace.

When the ceremony ended, we walked out as Mr. and Mrs. Gregory Gill, surrounded by bridesmaids, groomsmen, and daughters—all while Pharrell Williams' *Happy* played:

Clap along if you feel like a room without a roof...

Clap along if you feel like happiness is the truth...

It was the perfect ending to a perfect beginning.

After photos, we stopped at Starbucks before the reception. Our cups read *Bride* and *Groom*. Starbucks would become one of our favorite traditions—a place to pause, celebrate, and capture snapshots of our life together.

DIANA

We honeymooned in California, and I quickly learned something about Greg Gill: he seemed to know people everywhere we went! From city to city, friends and ministry connections welcomed us.

We visited the LA Dream Centre in Los Angeles,

Bethel in Redding, connected with a Bible school friend, and even went to a baseball game. It was a week of worship, laughter, sunshine, and new beginnings.

Only three months later, we took our first mission trip together—to the Philippines. At the wedding, a cowboy boot had been passed around and filled with money to support the trip. I didn't realize then how many more journeys we would take together, carrying God's love to the nations.

REFLECTION AND PRAYER

He said to them, "Go into all the world and preach the gospel to all creation." — **Mark 16:15**

1. Who do you know is standing beside you and supporting you? Write down their names.
2. How can you encourage someone else in their journey right now?
3. What is a song that has ministered deeply to you? Listen to it again and write down the lyrics.

PRAYER

Dear Lord,

Thank You for the people You've placed in my life to encourage and walk with me.

Thank You for new beginnings, for songs of joy, and for hope that rises again.

Help me to live each day with courage and to share Your love with others.

In Jesus' name, Amen.

CHAPTER 6
BLENDED = COUNSELLING

There are many schools of thought about counselling. Some people see it as weakness or something to be embarrassed about. Others recognize it as a lifeline. I once mentioned to someone that I had a counselling appointment, and their surprised reaction was, *"What do you need counselling for?"* Over the years, though, counselling has been a lifesaver. It has grounded us, given us perspective, and provided tools we could not have found on our own.

DIANA

Years ago, I went through a season of deep emotional healing. I write more about it in my book *You Call Me Beautiful*. At the time, my late husband, David, suggested counselling—and honestly, I was offended. He was right. It was exactly what I needed.

Walking into that counsellor's office wasn't easy. At first, I felt ashamed. My thoughts told me I was the only one who had ever felt this way. But the counsellor calmly explained that nothing I was going through was new. That may sound harsh, but it was actually freeing. My struggles weren't unique in the sense that I was *not alone*. Other people had walked this road before, and there were tools to help me walk it too.

I first sought counselling to navigate my relationship with my parents. Later, when David died, I went back to help me process my grief. Counselling reassured me that I wasn't losing my mind, and that the stages of grief—shock, denial, anger, deep sorrow—were part of a real process.

When Greg and I married, suddenly there were seven daughters in our blended family: my three girls, grieving the loss of their dad, and Greg's four daughters, learning to adjust to divorced parents. That was a huge shift. I told Greg we needed counselling because I had no idea what to do.

One of the most helpful things our counsellor said was this: *"Greg's daughters already have a mom and dad. You don't have to be their mother. You can be their friend."* That was a turning point. Instead of carrying the weight of being a second mom, I embraced being a safe, fun, supportive friend. It took pressure off me and created space for genuine connection.

Meanwhile, my daughters were still grieving their father. Accepting another man in my life was hard for them. Sometimes it still is. We had many honest talks as a couple about how to walk through all these changes together.

GREG

Going through separation and divorce, I spent a lot of hours in counselling. To be honest, I got tired of it, but those sessions gave me key insights. My counsellor helped me face the reality that I was no longer pastoring a local church. I had lost that dream, but I hadn't lost my calling. He reminded me of my love for travel and the many connections God had given me.

One day, God said: *"Greg, your dream was to pastor a church, but I want you to pastor the world."* That word shifted my perspective. My life didn't end with divorce. My ministry would just look different.

When Diana and I started our second chance, I knew we needed to sit down with a counsellor together. Those sessions gave us space to talk about our daughters, about how others viewed us, and about our own hurts that still needed healing. Counselling became a gift—a tool to keep us aligned, honest, and growing.

Even now, we use it as needed to stay healthy and grounded.

DIANA

I'll share one story from counselling that changed me. It's very personal, but I believe it may help you too.

One of my biggest struggles was how much I tried to financially help my daughters. I felt pressured to carry them through everything, especially since they had lost their dad, but this became a point of tension in our marriage.

During a session, our counsellor looked me in the eye and said: *"Show me your hands. Let me see the holes where you died on the cross for your kids."*

Tears rolled down my face. I understood immediately: I was not their Savior. Only Jesus is. As mothers, we want to rescue our kids from every pain, but there comes a point when we must let them go and allow them to figure things out. From that day, I began to reevaluate what helping really meant. It wasn't easy, but it was necessary—for them and for me.

REFLECTION AND PRAYER

> *Plans fail for lack of counsel, but with many advisers they succeed.* — **Proverbs 15:22 (NIV)**

1. Do you feel drawn—or resistant—to seeking counselling? Why?
2. If you went, what's the first thing you would want to share?
3. What key point in this chapter speaks most to your life right now?

PRAYER

Dear Lord,

Thank You for Your wisdom and for the people You place in our lives to guide us.

Thank You for the gift of counselling and the tools it provides.

Show me where I need to grow and give me the courage to take my next step.

In Jesus' name, Amen.

PART FOUR
ON MISSION & UPHEAVAL

CHAPTER 7
A WHOLE NEW WORLD

Everything was new: a new husband, a new wife, a new house, new friends, a new city—truly a whole new world.

DIANA

Before Greg came into my life, my world was quite small. When Dave and I were married, our vacations were usually at Bible camps. Dave would preach, and we would enjoy the beautiful scenery. I was a stay-at-home mom, so I could go on these trips while the girls were cared for at camp. We heard inspiring youth speakers—one of those events was where I first met Greg.

Dave and I once went on a mission trip to St. Lucia with 14 teenagers. Looking back, I see now it was training ground for what was ahead with Greg, though I didn't realize it at the time.

As I mentioned, a few months into our marriage, Greg and I traveled to the Philippines. There, I spoke at a ladies' conference. International speaking was something Greg had actually prophesied over me while we were still dating. I shared my story—how I became a widow and how God had carried me. Afterward, a woman came to me in tears. She too had lost her husband—11 years earlier. Her grief had been locked inside all that time, until that day. As I prayed with her, I realized the power of sharing my story. I could have stayed in my small town, curled up in grief. Instead, God was using my loss to bring life and healing to others.

Still working at the bank, I used my vacation time for both family holidays and mission trips. One of the most meaningful journeys was to Ukraine. Dave had started writing a book called *Getting Well at Being Sick* before he passed away. He wrote 11 chapters but didn't finish. On his deathbed, I promised him I would complete it. It took years, many tears, and Greg's encouragement, but I did it. Before our Ukraine trip, we had the book translated into Russian. Handing that book to people there—knowing Dave's words were now helping others—was powerful.

Later, we traveled to Australia, where I shared from my second book, *Hope in the Mourning*. After a Sunday service, two widows approached me. They said they had never thought a second chance was even possible. I told them, "You could be a gift to a man who needs a wife. Just as Greg and I are gifts to one another."

One memory stands out vividly. While Greg was on a mission trip to South Africa, I stayed back working. I would always call my Mum on the way to work, who had beginning stages of dementia. They were very short conversations, even 45 seconds was a long conversation. I told her that Greg was preaching in South Africa and changing the world! Then in a moment of clarity, she asked me, "Are you changing the world?" I was able to answer honestly, *"Yes, I am."* My books were reaching others, and I was climbing new mountains to bring encouragement to people in need.

GREG

Missions have always been in my heart. I've been to China 17 times, Trinidad and Tobago more than 20, Ukraine 12, and Africa several times. Traveling with Diana brought a whole new dimension. It was such a gift to have her by my side in the Philippines, Ukraine, and Australia.

When I travel overseas without her, I miss her deeply. That's part of the sacrifice of sharing the gospel, but knowing she is praying for me gives me strength.

One highlight was speaking in Ukraine about marriage. We separated the men and women into groups

—Diana spoke to the ladies, and I spoke to the men. Then we came together for questions and answers. For me, it was a dream come true—sharing our story, encouraging couples, and showing that God still has a plan even after loss.

DIANA

From my first marriage, I learned what it meant to truly care for a husband—in sickness and in health, for better or worse. Those vows were tested, but what began as duty became joy. God placed a deep desire in me to be a wife, and that calling still shapes me today.

Submitting to Greg doesn't make me less than him. It's a spiritual principle that carried me through my first marriage and now anchors my second chance. Being a wife is part of my purpose, and I count it an honour.

REFLECTION AND PRAYER

> *Take delight in the Lord, and he will give you the desires of your heart.* — **Psalm 37:4**

1. Where is a place you'd love to travel to?
2. What deep desires of your heart could you write down today?

3. What are some ways you've been stretched in your current journey?

PRAYER

Dear Lord,

Please show me the desires You've placed in my heart. Help me walk in Your plan with courage and strength. Calm my fears and lead me into each new journey You've prepared.

In Jesus' name, Amen.

CHAPTER 8
COVID AND MINIMALISM

Everyone remembers where they were when COVID began. For us, it was Phoenix, Arizona.

DIANA

We were finishing up a trip and stopped at Olive Garden. Every other table was closed. The next day, more tables were blocked off, and when we walked into Starbucks all the chairs were stacked on top of tables. You could only order and leave. It was surreal—like history unfolding before our eyes.

My boss texted me that when I returned home, I would have to quarantine for two weeks. No visitors. No shopping. Grocery orders were delayed three or four days.

Friends kindly left bags of food at our front and back doors.

With so much unexpected time at home, I decided to tackle the basement. Greg and I had boxes stacked from blending our lives, and it was time to sort through them. As I worked, I stumbled across YouTube videos on minimalism. Something clicked. I began decluttering cupboards, closets, and counters.

At one point, I realized I had 17 reusable Starbucks cups scattered across the kitchen! I kept my favorites and gave the rest away to coworkers. Their joy sparked mine. That's how minimalism took root in my life during COVID.

The process freed me—and prepared us. With a cleaner, simpler home, we even experimented with running our house as an Airbnb. It was extra income but also a lot of work. Still, it left our home lighter and uncluttered, like God was positioning us for what came next.

GREG

COVID hit me especially hard. My life revolved around travel and ministry. Suddenly, I was grounded. I had to reinvent how I ministered to the world.

I began hosting worship sessions at the piano, calling myself *The Quarantine Worshipper*. People tuned in from their homes and were blessed by the old hymns and songs of faith.

At the same time, I wrestled. Staying home messed with my head. I had meltdowns, moments of discouragement. But God opened a new door: broadcasting. With a green screen, new platforms, and encouragement from friends, I launched online programs to inspire others.

Another passion of mine is connecting people. I had hosted Ignite conferences for years, gathering pastors and leaders. During lockdown, I started gathering them on Zoom. From there, the Ignite Global Network was born—uniting pastors worldwide with encouragement and support.

When restrictions lifted, we held in-person conferences again—first in Calgary, then in San Antonio, Texas. At one event, my dear friend Pastor Warren Beemer opened his church and even hosted us for a BBQ at his beautiful home with his wife Faith. It was powerful to see the vision come alive in a whole new way.

DIANA

Even after travel reopened, minimalism stayed with us. We had rented our home out while on vacation in Florida, but when we returned, the place was a disaster. It was disheartening to see our sanctuary defiled. Thankfully, I had already decluttered, so restoring order was easier.

We also had some basement renovations underway to add value to the house. Greg and I often talked about downsizing. With the kids older, we didn't need so much space anymore.

GREG

One day, while waiting outside a store for Diana, I had a strong thought: *We should sell the house.* The market was hot, and houses were going fast. I called our realtor immediately, and he agreed to meet us the next morning.

When Diana came out of the store, I told her—and she jumped right in with excitement. There wasn't much left to do since the house was already clean and simplified. We even included our upright piano in the sale agreement. (Our realtor said he had never seen that before!)

Photos were taken Saturday night. By Sunday evening, the listing was live. By Monday, we already had showings. That night, we accepted an offer $20,000 above asking price. In just 24 hours, the house was sold.

It was both thrilling and nerve-racking, but we knew God was guiding every step.

REFLECTION AND PRAYER

> *Now to Him who is able to carry out His purpose and do superabundantly more than all that we dare ask or think—infinitely beyond our greatest prayers, hopes, or dreams—according to His power that is at work within us.* —
> **Ephesians 3:20 (AMP)**

1. What dreams has God placed in your heart?
2. What items could you release to lighten your load?
3. What step of faith is God asking you to take today?

PRAYER

Dear Lord,

Thank You for leading me into new seasons. Help me let go of what I don't need and trust You with what's next. May my life align with Ephesians 3:20—beyond what I could imagine.

In Jesus' name, Amen.

PART FIVE
GRIEF AGAIN & RESILIENCE

CHAPTER 9
LOVED ONES LOST

The beginning of 2022 brought loss. Greg's dad, **David Charles Thomas Gill**, passed away after a long battle with Huntington's disease. He had been unwell for more than ten years. Greg was meant to be away on a mission trip, but he canceled—and we could see God's hand in the timing, because he was able to attend the funeral. Surrounded by family, including all his grandchildren, he was honoured, even in the midst of COVID restrictions.

GREG

Losing my dad was huge. In some ways, the disease had taken him long before, but the funeral made the finality hit me in a new way. I had walked with Diana as she grieved before, and now it seemed to be my turn. I pressed on with our network, preparing for our San Antonio conference, but my heart was heavy.

At the same time, Diana and I had just sold our house. I was excited to tell my best friend, Pastor Warren Beemer, about the possibility of moving to San Antonio, which we had discussed a few months earlier. I tried calling him, but sometimes he only returned messages at two in the morning. Before I could connect with him, I left for a mission trip to Costa Rica—a scouting trip for future ministry.

On April 1, 2022, at about 11:00 p.m., I received the worst phone call of my life. A member of Pastor Warren's church told me he had been killed in a car accident. My brain and heart refused to believe it. I had to call Diana and tell her that my best friend, only 52 years old, was gone.

I scrambled to rearrange flights and get back to North America for a funeral in Louisiana, a memorial in San Antonio, and even to speak at Warren's church only a week after his passing. I was devastated, as were countless others. Warren was more than a pastor—he was a son, father, husband, and brother to so many.

But here we were, with a house sold and a dream of moving to San Antonio—to be near someone who was suddenly gone. It shook us to the core. It still does. That's why this book is dedicated to him. Warren had his own second chance, marrying his beautiful wife, Faith. His story inspired ours.

DIANA

The shock of Warren's death was overwhelming. We had been riding the high of selling the house, excited for the next adventure. Suddenly, everything shifted. That's what grief does—one phone call, one moment, and your life feels upside down.

I had known this shock before, but watching Greg go through it was heartbreaking. Grief comes in layers. It looks different when you lose a husband, a father, or a friend—but the ache is real every time.

On top of that, our sold house meant big changes. Part of the reason I had pushed for selling was to clear debt and finally deal with my one remaining rental property in Nipawin. What unfolded with that property was almost unbelievable.

My late husband, David, had chosen the renters in 2011, just before he died. For years, they were reliable. But eventually, the rent stopped. Months went by, stress piled up, and I lived ten hours away. Eviction proceedings were slow, tangled with COVID restrictions. Court papers were posted, texts exchanged, and sometimes small payments trickled in—enough to stall action.

Finally, after another long process, I pursued eviction

again. Just before the hearing, I received a shocking message on Facebook Messenger—from my renter's own account. At first I thought it was a cruel joke, but it was true: he had been murdered.

It was surreal. Eventually, with the help of a sheriff, I regained possession of the house, had it cleaned, and sold it to another landlord. With proceeds from the Calgary sale, I was able to pay off the debt completely. What had hung over me for more than a decade was finally lifted. Even in the chaos, God had been watching over every detail.

GREG

By mid-2022, it was time to move out of the home we had shared since our marriage. With no house to manage, Diana decided to take a leave from work, and together we traveled from June to September—to Trinidad and Tobago, Costa Rica, Australia, Dubai, and across the U.S. God's provision was unmistakable.

When we returned, we rented a brand-new apartment, preparing for a new season. Diana planned to return to work soon.

Then more news came. While ministering in Iowa that fall, I learned that my spiritual father, **Bill Carruthers**, had passed away. Bill had been my Bible school professor, mentor, and guide. He shaped my understanding of leadership and the Word. I had even dedicated my book *Much More* to him.

In 2022, I lost my father, my best friend, and my spiritual father. The grief reshaped me. Counselling became essential again as I sorted through the pain.

REFLECTION AND PRAYER

> *And we know [with great confidence] that God [who is deeply concerned about us] causes all things to work together [as a plan] for good for those who love God, to those who are called according to His plan and purpose.* —**Romans 8:28 (AMP)**

1. What grief moments have shaped your life?
2. Is there a loss you haven't fully grieved?
3. Write down five things you miss about your loved one.

PRAYER

Dear Lord,

Thank You for being near to the broken-hearted. Walk with me in my grief. Bring comfort, peace, and reminders of Your plan even in loss. Help me to honour the ones I love by living fully in Your purpose.

In Jesus' name, Amen.

CHAPTER 10
RENEWING OF VOWS AND REBUILDING

We made it! **August 15, 2024**—ten years married. How did the time go by so fast? In that decade, we faced ups and downs, traveled far and wide, and saw God's hand in our lives. Our second chance has always been a work in progress—but then again, so is life, and so is marriage. Marriage is sacred. It's meant for keeps. But when divorce and death happen, starting over is part of the journey. We are deeply thankful for these last ten years, and we believe the next decade will bring fresh strength, new foundations, and even more of God's call unfolding.

GREG

Ten years with Diana—it almost doesn't seem real. To go from the loneliness and despair I once felt, to now celebrating a decade with her, is something I treasure.

If there's one thing about our marriage, it's that we celebrate everything. Month after month, year after year, we've marked anniversaries big and small. On the 15th of each month, I'd bring Diana roses—sometimes a dozen, sometimes two dozen if Costco had them. For every occasion, I'd buy not just one card but three, four, sometimes even five. Hallmark became my second home. Along with the cards, I'd stop at Crave Cupcakes—Diana's favorite—and bring home a box of them for us to enjoy.

For our tenth anniversary, I wanted to do something more. I wanted to **renew our vows**. So, with the help of family and friends, we put together an evening ceremony and dinner. Our dear friend Mark Griffin officiated. It was a night of love, prayer, and gratitude—not waiting for 25 or 50 years to celebrate, but choosing to honour what God had done right now.

DIANA

I can still remember being impatient when Greg and I were dating, wondering when we would finally marry. Now, here we are—ten years later. Through every challenge of building a second-chance life together, we've celebrated each step.

Just before our vow renewal, we had celebrated Greg's oldest daughter's wedding. It was beautiful, and Greg's mom was able to come and help with our renewal dinner, even sorting out the menu. For the ceremony, we chose to write **new vows** for each other.

Here are mine:

Bishop Greg, I promise to love you when you don't feel loved, to honour you when you don't feel honoured, and to be your biggest cheerleader. In these ten years we've faced death, celebrated life, welcomed six grandchildren with one more on the way, and walked with seven daughters as they've grown into relationships, engagements, and marriages. Conquering life with you has been an adventure. You've made me fly—on planes, yes, but also in life, into dreams I never thought I'd achieve. I believe the next ten years will surpass our imagination. (Ephesians 3:20)

I promise to answer your texts, your WhatsApp, your Messenger, and your phone calls—because you never stop finding ways to say you love me, miss me, or care about me, no matter where you are in the world. Thank you for believing in me, for loving me so deeply, for spoiling me with trips, dinners, coffee (even when it keeps me awake). I love you.

And Greg's vows to me:

Diana, I am so thankful that God brought you into my life. You are a gift from Him—more than I could ask or imagine (Ephesians 3:20). Of all we have accomplished these past ten years, the thing I value most is the time I get with you, just us. I'm thankful for your passion for God and people, for the way you light up over little joys like chocolate, breakfast in bed, or Starbucks runs. I'm thankful for the special touches you add to life, and how you always know what I need. Most of all, I am thankful for your love and support.

I promise to keep loving you better, to encourage you, to stretch you, to lead you, and to walk with you into all that God has for us. I am a blessed man. You are God's gift to me. I love you, Diana.

Neither of us realized until that night that we had both chosen the same verse—**Ephesians 3:20**. It felt like God confirming His promise over us again.

GREG

After celebrating our vows with family and friends, I headed back out on a mission—this time to Australia and New Zealand. Ministry continues, but this renewal gave me fresh strength.

Earlier that summer, we had felt God call us to plant a

church. I asked Diana if she would stand with me in this, because I didn't want to step forward without her agreement. She said yes, and together we began.

We started with five people—friends searching for a church home. But we needed a space. Our apartment was too small. Then Diana reminded me of a man I had met, the head of a school for children with special needs. I hadn't spoken to him in some time, but I texted him to ask if he might have space for us.

He replied immediately: *"Let's meet for lunch Monday."* At lunch, I shared our vision. He offered us the school library. When I asked the cost, he said: *"How about $1.00 for the whole year?"*

I couldn't believe it. $1.00? Only God. Later, when I told a friend about it, he sent me a dollar by e-transfer, insisting he wanted to pay our first year's rent. We laughed, but we also rejoiced at God's goodness.

Ignite Global Church was born—on *Prince of Peace Way*, no less. Another sign we were on the right path.

This new season means less traveling and more time home with Diana. It's a shift, but one we both welcome. Our faith is stirred for what lies ahead—for those who need Christ, not just for believers shifting from church to church.

REFLECTION AND PRAYER

> *Behold, how good and how pleasant it is*
>   *For brothers to dwell together in unity!*
>   *It is like the precious oil poured on the head,*
>   *Running down on Aaron's beard,*
>   *Down upon the collar of his robe.*
>   *It is as if the dew of Hermon were falling on Mount Zion.*
>   *For there the Lord bestows his blessing,*
>   *Even life forevermore.*
>   **—Psalm 133:1–3**

1. What in your life deserves celebrating today?
2. What verse captures your life vision right now?
3. Do you find yourself closer to God after this journey—or is this a new beginning with Him?

A PRAYER OF SALVATION

Dear Lord Jesus,

Thank You for dying on the cross for my sins. Please forgive me—I confess I am a sinner in need of You. Lead me in Your plan for my life, even after all I've been through. I place my future in Your hands.

In Jesus' name, Amen.

PART SIX
YOUR SECOND CHANCE

CHAPTER 11
WHAT DOES YOUR SECOND CHANCE LOOK LIKE?

In the book of Ruth, we meet three women bound by grief—Naomi and her two daughters-in-law, Orpah and Ruth. Naomi had lost her husband, and after ten years, both of her sons also died. Suddenly, all three women were widows. Their world was turned upside down.

> "Now Elimelek, Naomi's husband, died, and she was left with her two sons... After they had lived there about ten years, both Mahlon and Kilion also died, and Naomi was left without her two sons and her husband." —**Ruth 1:3–5**

If anyone needed a second chance, it was these women.

Naomi urged her daughters-in-law to return to their homes so they could remarry:

> "Go back, each of you, to your mother's home. May the Lord show you kindness... May the Lord grant that each of you will find rest in the home of another husband." —**Ruth 1:8–9**

Naomi was saying: *Your story isn't over. You can have another beginning.*

Ruth chose to stay with Naomi, and her faithfulness led to a redemption story that still echoes today. God brought Boaz into her life, and together they had a son.

> "Praise be to the Lord, who this day has not left you without a guardian-redeemer... He will renew your life and sustain you in your old age. For your daughter-in-law, who loves you and who is better to you than seven sons, has given him birth." —**Ruth 4:14–15**

Naomi, once bitter and empty, now held a grandson in her arms. Ruth, once widowed and displaced, was now part of the lineage of Jesus Christ.

This is the power of a second chance: sorrow turned to joy, emptiness turned to legacy, and brokenness turned to redemption.

Your story may not look like Naomi's or Ruth's, but God's promise is the same—He is the Redeemer who writes second chances into our lives. Earthly sorrow is temporary. Eternity is secure. Trust Him with the details, even when nothing makes sense.

Because sometimes your second chance is already unfolding—you just haven't seen the ending yet.

PASTOR WARREN'S SECOND CHANCE

Our dear Pastor Warren Beemer, to whom this book is dedicated, had walked through deep sorrow. Like Greg, he experienced the heartbreak of divorce after many years of marriage. These two men, raised with similar values and callings, found themselves navigating the pain of starting over.

Warren longed for companionship again, but he didn't leave it to chance—he made a list of what he believed the Lord would give him in a new wife. His list was detailed: she would be younger than him, from Louisiana, able to cook authentic Louisiana food, have dark hair, a tattoo, and a few life experiences that would make her relatable to the broken and the lost he had such a heart for. It was as though God had already given him a picture of her.

Then he met Faith—the one chosen to love him unconditionally and to share the next chapter of his life. She embraced Warren's two beautiful daughters and quickly became an important part of their lives.

One day, on a family trip to Disney World in Orlando

—Warren's favorite place—he asked Faith to marry him. Right in front of the Magic Kingdom castle, with his daughters by his side, Faith said yes. A month and a half after standing in our wedding party and giving a touching tribute, Warren and Faith stood together in Baton Rouge, Louisiana, and said their vows.

Warren often spoke of the promise that God would give him a son. When Faith became pregnant, they were overjoyed. Sadly, they lost their first baby, a heartache that tested their faith. But God brought healing, and in time, they welcomed a beautiful baby boy, Maxamos. For Warren's daughters, having a baby brother was a joy, and Faith, who later adopted the girls as her own, became a true gift from God to their family.

Their love story, however, was cut short. On April 1, 2022, Warren went home to be with the Lord at the age of 52. His passing left a void in the lives of his family, friends, and all who loved him. Though we don't understand why his time here on earth was shortened, we hold to the truth that God still has a plan for Faith, for Maxamos, and for Warren's daughters.

Warren lived fully, loved deeply, and poured himself into others. His motto was simple yet powerful: *"It's a GOOD DAY!"* And that is how he would want us to carry on—trusting the Lord with every detail, living with joy and purpose, and making the most of the second chances we are given.

CONCLUSION AND SUMMARY

TEN TIPS FOR YOUR SECOND CHANCE

1. **Get Healed** – Do all that you can to heal your heart through the redemption of Jesus Christ and His death on the cross.
2. **Stop and Reflect** – Take time to notice what is happening around you. Loneliness is real, but God is near to the lonely and desires to speak to you.
3. **Take Heart** – Have courage and faith. God has you, and He wants more for your life than you can imagine.
4. **Trust the Lord** – *"Trust in the Lord with all your heart and lean not on your own understanding; in*

all your ways acknowledge Him, and He will make your paths straight." (Proverbs 3:5–6)

5. **Write It Down** – Be bold. Write down the qualities you desire in a future husband or wife and trust God with your list.
6. **Find Your Circle** – Surround yourself with people who believe in you, encourage you, and will pray for you on your journey.
7. **Seek Wise Counsel** – Don't be afraid to reach out to a counsellor or coach to work through your next steps and heart issues with honesty and openness.
8. **Let Go of the Past** – Release what has been and press forward into what is ahead. It may not look the way you imagined, but God still has a plan.
9. **Learn From Others** – Be encouraged by the testimonies of others and remember that God holds you securely in the palm of His hand.
10. **Celebrate the Small Things** – Rejoice in what God is doing, even in the little details. Trust His promise: *"For I know the plans I have for you,"* declares the Lord, *"plans to prosper you and not to harm you, plans to give you hope and a future."* (Jeremiah 29:11)

CONCLUSION AND SUMMARY

As we come to the close of this book, we want to thank you for journeying through these pages with us. Our prayer is that God has spoken hope, healing, and encouragement into your life.

Maybe you are in the middle of your own second chance, or perhaps you are standing in faith with a friend who needs one. Wherever you find yourself today, know this: God always has a plan. Life can be unpredictable, but His love is steadfast, His timing is perfect, and His faithfulness never fails.

Hold onto hope. Believe again. Your second chance is closer than you think.

FINAL PRAYER OF BLESSING

Heavenly Father,

I thank You for every reader who has walked through these pages. You see their heart, their past, and their future. I pray that You would pour out fresh hope, renewed faith, and a deep assurance that You are with them in every season of life.

Bless them with courage to step into their second chance, with wisdom to follow Your leading, and with peace that surpasses all understanding. Surround them with people who will lift them up, encourage them, and walk with them on the journey ahead.

I declare Your promises over their life—that they will

prosper, that they will not be harmed, and that You will give them hope and a future (Jeremiah 29:11). May they see Your goodness in the land of the living and may their story bring glory to Your name.

In Jesus' name,

Amen.

ABOUT THE AUTHORS

Bishop Greg D. Gill and Lady Diana Gill have been married for 11 years. They have experienced both death and divorce and pushed forward. Combined they have seven beautiful daughters, seven awesome grandchildren and some amazing son in laws. They have both authored other books individually but this is their first book together.

ALSO BY
BISHOP GREG D. GILL
AND
DIANA E. GILL

DIANA E. GILL'S BOOKS

Getting Well at Being Sick by David C. Hamata

Hope in the Mourning: A Journey Into Grief

You Call Me Beautiful: A Journey of Healing

BISHOP GREG D. GILL'S BOOKS

I Will Not: Pursuing the Path to Perseverance

Much More: Unleashing the Holy Spirit Made

for More: Living in the Purposes of God *Please*

visit www.myeim.org *for more information.*

www.ingramcontent.com/pod-product-compliance
Lightning Source LLC
Chambersburg PA
CBHW030657230426
43665CB00011B/1137